How To Meditate Like A Boss

Chris Perkins

Copyright © 2017 Chris Perkins

Illustrations by Chris Perkins copyright CPPS
How to Meditate Like A Boss and all related characters and elements
TM of and CPPS
How to Meditate Like A Boss Publishing Rights Chris Perkins
All rights reserved. Published by CP Production Studios Publishing,
Publishers since 2000

No part of this publication may be reproduced,
Stored in a retrieval system, any form or by any means, electronic,
mechanical, photocopying, recording, or otherwise, without the
written permission of the publisher.
For more information regarding permission, write to CP Production
Studios Attention:
Permissions Department

Perkins, Christopher How To Meditate Like A Boss / by Chris Perkins.
Summary: Connect with your inner-self and discover who you really
are.

[1. Meditation- Non-Fiction 2. Religion – Meditation]

Printed in the U.S.A. First American Edition November 27th, 2017

We try to produce the most beautiful books possible, and we are
extremely concerned about the impact of our manufacturing process
on the forests of the world and the environment as a whole.
Accordingly, we made sure that all of the paper we used contains 30%
post-consumer recycled fiber. We love those who care and that is
what we're all about!

CP Production Studios where dreams come true

DEDICATION

To everyone who wants to better themselves

CP PRODUCTION STUDIOS
WHERE DREAMS COME TRUE

Contents

Knowing Who you are 2

Staying away from negATIve words 7

Your Motivation 11

Bad Meditation 16

Reactions to the body 21

addictions 27

Completion 32

ABOUT THE AUTHOR 35

SUBSCRIBE TO MY WEBSITE

www.creativechris.weebly.com

ACKNOWLEDGMENTS

I want to thank everyone for taking a step forward to progress in their lives.

Before we get into how to meditate like a boss. I want you to relax. Now as you relax, I want you to think of a time you were happy. Connect with the emotion. Next, I want you to breathe in and Breathe out. As you breathe out, I want you to say, "I am smart, I am intelligent, I meditate like a boss"! Good now that you got that down packed. We can now begin. This is the start of your legacy! You will become what you say you want to become and achieve whatever your heart desires. Before we begin let's start with the basics.

Chris Perkins

KNOWING WHO YOU ARE

Do you know who you are? Don't panic! Most people don't but, do worry because time is fading, and you need to be in the position you were called to be in! What if you were the person that was supposed to be running the store you work at, or what if you were the one that was supposed to get the promotion! So, that you can have extra money to provide for your family or for yourself if you don't have one.

Many of us miss out on opportunity because we don't know who we are! A lot of people miss out on the opportunity because they feel they don't have a support system. The question is, do you need one? Yes and no, the reason you need one now! is that you do not know who you are! Meditation helps us connect with our inner-self and enlightens us to better. People see us different, more things will begin to happen in your life because the more you meditate the more you know the inner you.

Meditation brings prosperity! The question is, why?

What is prosperity? the state of being prosperous.

Meaning success!

"Oh, I want to be successful"!

Do you know who you are?

A person may say, I want a man or woman who I can marry that loves me for me. The question is, Do you love yourself? I want this promotion but, I don't know if I'm good enough or they might not like me or John Doe is way better than me anyways! The question is,

Do you know who you are?

Meditation helps you find yourself. Connecting with the source above. Connecting with your inner-self telling yourself that you are bright, that you are intelligent and good looking. I am who I say I am because this is my body and I do what I tell it to do?

STAYING AWAY FROM NEGATIVE WORDS

You will be surprised at how many people I see every day, say, at least one negative thing about themselves. The question is why? Many times, people will say words that other people say about them.

"Dude, you are so stupid, why did you do that?"

Later down the road! You make a mistake and you call yourself stupid. Why? Because you allowed a negative response to become your decree. So automatically, because you did not come against that negative word or you didn't go into meditation, you cause it to have an effect on your life. Now every time you make a mistake, you call yourself stupid. Not a question is,

do you know who you are?

Many of you who are reading this book have kids, and I know you get angry at them sometimes, but you cannot use any negative words. Words are powerful, words set the course of life. But a word! Can affect a child worse than a parent! Why? Because child your child looks up to you. Now if you call this child stupid and you say that he won't be successful or you say you're just lazy. You cause that child to act in that type way. Again, words are a. Powerful and words set the course of life. The question, I ask you once more.

Do you know who you are?

10

YOUR MOTIVATION

Who motivates you? Do you motivate yourself? This is a question if you do not motivate yourself it will cause you to rely on others. How can you let someone else motivate you and you can't even motivate yourself? It shows your lack of being in tune with ones-self. Your body is seeking it because it thirst's the need to relax and to be whole.

Oh, it is too much work to meditate a person might say!

Then, you one who does not seek to be successful and to have a peaceful life. Therefore, you will continue to be the person who quenches for the thirst of meditation. But, because you are here you are telling yourself I want to better. Which is a good sign so give yourself a PAT on the back! You are steps closer to becoming a boss in meditation.

Repeat after me,

"I meditate like a boss because I am a boss"

say it three times so that your mind will understand. Meditation helps you motivate yourself by keeping your levels high. You are now in tuned to your inner-self. You can now see who you truly are. Why? Meditation surpasses blinders we all walk with on in life. Think of the entire world walking with a blindfold on and you're the only one with it off. That means you're awaken and you are not connected to the system that was leading you to destruction! Meaning you now awaken to speak over anything in your life and it will come to pass. When you were a blinded object connected to the systems cord you lost your identity of knowing who you are. Things always happen spiritually then natural. Once you connect with your spiritual self you will cause a significant impact in the natural.

Chris Perkins

BAD MEDITATION

People are curious just like a child. When you tend to do things they usually don't do out of the norm. YouTube can be a reliable source for you but, it can also be a negative source for you as well. Many will show you the way to meditate but, does it mean it's the right way. Performing rituals and words that you cannot understand the meaning of is not a good thing to do. Speaking positive and connecting yourself with the one above is. You can say things positive about yourself and speak those things into existence don't do extra! That will switch things around like knocking out positive and bringing in negative. That's is a big NO NO!

You want to be successful keep it simple!

List of signs that tell you that you are doing your meditation wrong. One through seven.

1. Constant Thinking

Stop thinking and relax. That's the biggest key.

2. You're not relaxed

A lot of people tend to skip the first step, which is to relax.

3. You're surrounded by distraction.
    - Yes, you can listen to music and sounds of nature.
    - Placing yourself where there is continuous walk flow in your home is a bad idea.
4. You're not feeling anything

    -it is a must that you should feel some type of vibration and connection from the source above
5. Not focusing on what you're truly meditating for.

    -Stay focused

6. Not hearing

    -you should hear something while in meditation. Such as guidance in your life.

7. You should be seeing results immediately after you completed meditation.

These are key points and you must listen to them. So, that you can meditate correctly. Remember, meditating correctly means, faster results.

REACTIONS TO THE BODY

What happens to the body while in meditation. Ten benefits listed below.

Stress is a state of mental or emotional strain or tension resulting from adverse or very demanding circumstances. A lot of things can cause stress like work, relationships, school, three of those things listed can cause an extreme tension of stress. The scary part about it is, that a lot of people don't know they have it. Stress can cause problems in the body. The body doesn't need the stress! Get rid of it by doing meditation.

Sleep problems, a lot of people have stressed. It causes loss of sleep. Which is bad, we all need rest to reenergize for a fresh new day. Meditation enhances your sleep, which is a cure rather than taking any sleep medication the doctor gives you.

A lot of times the medicine doctors give you affect your pineal gland which meditation enhances.

Meditation also improves your outer look. It increases your sex appeal men or women will be more into you. You will notice them more, the ones you didn't notice before.

Meditation gives you a sense of purpose. (The beauty in the sound of that). Meaning you are steps closer to knowing who you truly are!

Meditation opens your mind and helps you focus and improves your awareness keeps you alert. It's like being on marijuana which studies show that it helps connect you to a higher level of yourself. A lot of people would agree to this but, you have to realize that yes you can use marijuana and other ways besides smoking it which I prefer and yes it can help you reach that level a lot faster but, people tend to abuse marijuana which ends up turning into a drug, rather than a cure for something.

Meditation improves your happiness. If you are depressed and always upset about what's going on or just having a difficult day, **MEDITATE** it helps trust me.

If you're in a relationship, it improves your sexual life and your connection with your partner. You begin to connect with that person both spiritually and naturally. People who lack this should pursue in meditating. Join some classes and do it with a group of people so that connection can be even stronger.

ADDICTIONS

You cannot read this unless you truly want to stop at whatever you're addicted to. If you must please continue reading. I must say that if you do not want to change think about this section later and come back when you're ready! If you are ready, then continue reading. First, grab a pen and a piece of paper. This step is the most important so please read carefully. Once you have grabbed both items, I

Chris Perkins

want you to write down all of the addictions you have. Good now that you have completed that task you are steps closer to getting rid of your addiction. Look at what you wrote. Get a lighter and burn it in the sink where you have access to water, or in the backyard. Somewhere safe, please! Once you have completed doing that, go to a quiet place to meditate. Breathe in, breathe out, turn on some soothing music. Think of a place you always wanted to be if it's with your family, your favorite place or a dream vacation. Think of it! Without you thinking of your addiction. Say,

"I no longer have the addiction to (Your addiction) and No longer will I feed its appetite! Keep saying it trust me it's going to hurt it's an addiction. It craves to be feed but, you must fight to overcome.

Remember you must fight to overcome.

There was a girl by the name of Anne who had an addiction but, she blames her addiction on past instances that happen in her life. Many people in the world resemble that same problem. Someone has caused harm to you in your life and to someone you love. So, decide to blame yourself for whatever happened. The key to meditation is to forgive. You want to be a boss at meditation forgive those who have caused harm to you in your life. That way meditation will be easier for you. Forgive and meditate, now when I say forgive I also mean you. The reason you have an addiction is that you hate yourself for whatever reason and a lot of us don't even realize it. Trust me if you are not a person who forgives. Go somewhere by yourself and say it to yourself. You will begin to cry and not know why but, you are getting even closer to becoming a boss at meditation. You are intelligent, you are beautiful, and you deserve to live because your inner-self and the one above is telling you that. You just have been wearing ear muffs and blindfolds this whole time and you were connected to the systems cord. You are now free, I can feel it your steps closer to becoming a boss a meditation. Repeat those words. I am one step closer to becoming a boss at meditation.

Chris Perkins

COMPLETION

Congratulations you completed on how to be a boss in meditation. How do you feel? Now, just because this chapter says completion doesn't technically mean we are finished. You still have one more thing to do. While holding this book in your hand I want you to walk in front of the mirror, look at yourself and say fifty things good about yourself and when you say it. I want you to feel it with emotion. I don't care who's around because this is a healing process. You want better for yourself and for your family and if that is important to you. Then continue, Now once you're done share your experience with a friend or family member. Give them the book for Christmas or as a gift so they can change and become a better person as well. Remember to speak it into existence. "I meditate like a boss" You will begin to discover even the more. WHO YOU REALLY ARE. SO, I ASK YOU AGAIN DO YOU KNOW WHO YOU ARE?

ABOUT THE AUTHOR

Chris Perkins is a bestselling author and continues to express meditation throughout the world.

Please leave a review on Amazon and tell us your answer. Do you know who you are?

www.ingramcontent.com/pod-product-compliance
Lightning Source LLC
LaVergne TN
LVHW051529070426
835507LV00023B/3382